a beautiful composition of broken

a beautiful composition of broken

r.h. Sin

Andrews McMeel
PUBLISHING®

intro.

i took my expectations
and buried them all
at the bottom of the sea
because i alone
was never brave enough
to dive that deep

i took my pain
the anguish
and turned it into power
i found more of myself
in the loneliest of hours

i used my tears to create rivers
for my boat
on disappointment and betrayal
i float
i float

i took your absence
as a sign to move on
now the melody has changed
and i sing a new song

my heart, broken blue
my mind split in two
and yet i gained peace
at the loss of you

i took the heartache
and learned a lesson
i began after we ended
you leaving was my blessing

a love worth keeping.

i wish
i wish
for love like this
a love like summer
being kissed by the sun

a love like winter
hugged and covered with snow
a love like the night
being lit by the moon's glow

i pray

i pray

that this never fades away

many claims of being in love

but none of them ever stay

i hope

i hope

i rely on our love

i rely on your heart

i wish, i hope

i pray we never part

devil, defeated.

i believe that the devil

takes a bow

when we lose

delighted by our mistakes

and the bad things that we choose

delighted by our pain

the devil does rejoice

defeated by our demons

the serpents who steal

our voice

but deep within the darkness

there's a light that we find

a strength, a power

something to free our mind

something to free our soul

we go to war to fight for peace

bruised and battered

and yet we find a way

to bring the devil to his knees

3:29:50 p.m.

what is it that you love about him
is it the way he lets you down
incapable of lifting you up

is it the way your heart breaks
when he says something
that shatters your self-esteem

is it the fact he never shows up
when you need him

tell me again
what is there to love
about a man who doesn't love you

from pain, came this.

my horror story began with you

and ended with your departure

the confusion and the pain of it all

turned me into an author

a poet for the poets

a voice for the voiceless

i speak for the weak

i rally for the strong

at 7:22 p.m., to my love.

will you miss me when i'm gone

what will the room sound like

without my voice

what will the room smell like

without my scent

my random sayings

my cough

my laughter

me yelling when angry

the sound of me weeping

when sad

my smile

will you miss it

my lips, my tongue

the kissing

when i vanish into air

will you care

will you grieve

will you stay here

in this home

or will my absence

make you leave

all i ask is that you remember

and that you never forget about me

November '13.

lonely like the winter

i searched for warmth

and found nothing but cold air

with nothing but pain living there

seeds that grow.

the suffering will make you strong
the pain will help you grow

you haunt the devil.

transforming heartache into lessons

refusing to remain down

when falling

not afraid to stare

your abusers in the eyes

the devil fears women like you

soft light.

your softness

is your gift

your sensitivity

is beautiful

most of who you are

will go unappreciated

by men

who don't deserve you

anima I.

loving yourself

will save your soul

anima II.

you will find your soul mate

when you fall for yourself first

life jacket.

you can't save the person
who refuses to appreciate
or acknowledge your effort

this is what i had to learn
this is what i've come to accept

a terrible terror of love I.

it's scary

how you can do

so much for someone

and yet they'd rather focus

on what you don't do

the false remains.

i edit the memories of you

pretending you thought more of me

than what you actually did

i'm much happier

lying to myself

about us

mobile distractions.

should've held my hand more

instead of your phone

a restless nightmare.

my mental walls are crashing down on me

wide awake in this nightmarish thought

please save me from my own mind

everything 7:22.

she is both complex

and easy to love

mating souls 7:22.

give me eternal promises

an infinite love

and i'll give you mine

whatever helps.

you have been strong for so long

cry if you need to

scream if it helps

much more.

you are tougher than your demons

you are greater than the pain

both ways.

take a lover

who will choose you

like you choose them

begin again, again.

you're cold
but you'll love again

when snow melts
the flowers grow again

learned lessons.

gather the sorrow

and let it teach you

collect the heartache

and heal

different :22.

i fell in love with your strange

my heart fell for your crazy

in your lips.

with one kiss

you make the madness

of the world

disappear

removing you.

screaming fuck you

into the wind on a chilly night

the moon is full

as i empty myself of you

retrieve self.

sometimes i wish i could get back

all of myself that i wasted on you

internal blaze.

the memory of you

burns like a flame

in my skull

love :22.

but when you touch me
i remember how it feels
to feel okay

the lonely ones.

you're trying to be everything
to someone who doesn't care
for you

more lessons.

having my heart broken
helped me understand the true weight
of holding on to the wrong person

the terror.

you're terrified of feeling complete

you have a fear of becoming whole

and so you've accepted

being broken

we, like flowers.

too soon

the flowers dry up

then die without warning

the depth.

there is so much more to you

than your reflection in the mirror

you are too deep for the understanding

of shallow souls

<u>1:25.</u>

you are forgiven
but there is no longer
a space provided here
for you

mid-December lesson.

not everyone you love

deserves your patience

not everyone you love

deserves your fight

not everyone you love

deserves your heart

not everyone you love

understands that love

late December love.

we're conditioned to love

what we know

and if all we know

is pain

this is what we tend

to choose

before '13.

i couldn't stay

my heart was too heavy

for your hands

my mind was too complex

for you to comprehend

and my soul was never yours

to keep

early mourning.

in mourning

i found truth

in mourning

i found clarity

in mourning

i found peace

because i understand.

there's a black hole

where your heart used to be

and i won't judge you for that

less.

i give minimal attention
to those who do nothing
but tear me down emotionally
until i eventually
give them nothing at all

among the living.

i went on living
even when i felt like
i couldn't anymore
even when i felt like
i didn't want to

ongoing.

your love is infinite

find someone who understands this

the after.

in order to heal properly

you must walk away

from what broke you

a grave love.

for so long
i was dating death
falling deep into a grave
that looked like love

tender beginnings.

who were you

when you first fell in love

a tender, timid heart

a soul in search of longing

vulnerable and beautiful

unprepared for heartache

the first one we love

is often the one

to teach us about pain

Monday after 6.

awkwardness and tension

short questions met with short answers

communicating without communication

or comprehension

no understanding

we are no longer

who we were before

neither friend nor foe

nothing, no one

just two strangers

who used to know

one another

a love i hate.

a flame made weak by lies
a love that fell flat after betrayal
a heart, broken down
by the very person who promised
to protect it

you were never my forever
you were only my end

Raymond's literary grave.

you were never as good

as you pretended to be

something short of what i am

and so you're jealous of me

growing green with envy

your soul is undone

you've had many losses in your life

you may count this as one

blitz.

with love comes several failures

many attempts met unsuccessfully

no start.

and so we search for endless love
in places where it'll never begin

battle tested.

a woman is a warrior

with infinite strength

twenty 2.

you began to talk like me
your facial expressions like my own
this is when i knew you were mine

the sorrow.

there's nothing more confusing

and painful to a woman

than being told that she's amazing

by a man who treats her like

she's not good enough to commit to

and the saddest part of it all

is that this woman

will fight to prove her value

to the one man

who doesn't even deserve her

the fight.

the fight to prove yourself

to someone who doesn't deserve you

is a losing battle

what is there to achieve

when the one you want

has nothing to give you in return

where is the benefit

in going to war for someone

who'd rather fight against you

instead of beside you

the questions I.

here you are, alone

taken but alone

in a relationship

that feels like a big

question mark

constantly wondering

and wandering off

into a thick silence

struggling to find the words

at odds with your own heart

what should feel good

has become painful to bear

you wear sadness well

but i can tell that you're tired

you're fed up, you want out

the wrong mate I.

being with the wrong person

is a time suck

loving someone

who refuses to love you

drains the heart

the soul becomes weary

the longer you stay

the opportunity to find

your soul mate

becomes greatly reduced

the wrong mate II.

real love arrives

when the heart

no longer clings

to the wrong love

real love can only be found

when the heart

no longer searches

for it in the wrong places

the problem.

there's the problem

you say you want love

but you've settled for someone

who treats you like

they hate you

the silent.

you can tell, you just know
you always do

no man on this earth
could keep secrets
from a woman like you

but i hate this idea
of knowing everything
and saying nothing
i hate this idea
of a woman being silent

the realization.

here's the thing
i realized that being loved
by you
was completely overrated

the lies.

sure enough

an honest love exists

but we're too busy

entertaining the lies told

by the people we think love us

the choice.

i didn't quit

i simply chose myself

instead of continuing to try

for someone who wouldn't

try for me

the better.

placing you behind me

pushed me closer

to something better

the thought.

i like to think

that all the pain

and heartache

is simply preparing me

for a love that heals

the craving.

sometimes the love you crave

can't be found in the person you want

and wanting someone is not enough

to have them love you

the women.

thank you to the women
who never get a thank-you
thank you to the women
who never get acknowledged

thank you for your softness
thank you for your toughness
thank you for your strength
your endurance
your ability to take pain
and transform it into power

the ability.

i admire your ability to fight

i admire your ability to go to war

for all the things

you know you deserve

the bridge.

sadly, i watched from the other side

as you burned the one bridge

that you never deserved to cross

the further.

you went missing

when i longed for you the most

while my heart didn't grow fonder

my mind grew further

how quickly i went from sadness

to feeling nothing at all

the coffee shops.

there's this thing about coffee shops
for the life of me
it's hard to put into words
the experience my soul feels
when all of my morning thrills
sit at the bottom of that circular
ceramic cup

the atmosphere
the people
the lovers sitting hand in hand
the friends, laughing silently
me, gazing into the eyes of my lover
speaking without saying words

sipping slowly
the sweet life
the brown hue of enjoyment
and delight
sitting near the window
in search of the perfect light

the tights you wear.

wrapped around both thighs

black hues and heather grays

beginning at the waist

ending just at the ankles

forcing me to pay homage

to your curves

the days.

30-plus days

without hearing the voice

of my nephew

30-plus days

of frustration and disregard

30-plus days

i was angry in the beginning

30-plus days

i'm more accepting of it now

it's been 30-plus days

of missing this interaction

30-plus days

of wondering what the fuck happened

30-plus days

one day i'll tell him about it

30-plus days

i'll write about it for now

the return.

i should hate you

but even then

that would be way more

than you actually deserve

and so i'll give you nothing

to match the nothing

you gave me in return

the becoming.

for so long
the only one deserving
of me
was myself

for so long
i transformed
into everything i needed

for too long
i've been disappointed
by people who were never capable
of becoming
what i've always been
struggling to find a love in others
that i could easily cultivate
on my own

the internet.

everything is fake deep nowadays
life plagued by internet gurus
teaching about a love they've
yet to provide to the women
in their lives

fooling these hurt women
who follow in search of clarity
but confusion is all they're selling
stringing together words to create sentences
to manipulate the masses
of women who wish for nothing more
than to be loved and cherished

this hurts me . . .

the social media.

don't drink their water

don't sip from their wells

show no interest in what they offer

stop buying what they're selling

silence their lies

by not listening at all

remove them from your timelines

block their accounts

don't repost

don't like

don't bookmark

don't screenshot

beware of deceitful people

exploiting your vulnerabilities

while filling their pockets

by your desire to have the quick fix

for your heartache that they've promised

to provide but never do

the questions II.

are you tired

are you weary

are you unhappy

have you accepted

this fate

have you allowed

them to destroy you

have you settled

for this type of relationship

knowing that you could have

done better

or are you unaware

that something better exists

the cold.

next to you felt lonely

next to you felt cold

your presence felt like absence

your love felt like pain

the nights.

we move on

or at least we think we do

hiding our pain with a smile

locking away the memories

behind the bars of our subconscious

but the things

we force ourselves to forgot

creep up beside us

in the middle of the night

the questions III.

are you awake

i often wonder

have you thought of me

like i think of you

is this as painful for you

as it's been for me

i'm tired of needing you

suffering from the realization

that you never needed me

wasn't ready.

we're young, we're just kids

setting ourselves on fire

for tainted love

placing labels of forever

on temporary people

we're so young

and yet we're so hurt

we're just teens

acting like adults

but no one taught us

how to love correctly

no one prepared us

for this

version of disappointment

and we fall in love

before we're ready

mold.

pain shapes a woman
into a warrior

truly.

a man who truly loves you

chooses you every day

he chooses you forever

zero explanation.

you don't have to explain

why you left

to the person who made you leave

quiet.

don't respond when you're angry

you end up saying things

you don't actually mean

you end up hurting people

you're not supposed to hurt

you end up saying things

you'll never be able to take back

12 is hell.

at midnight

you haunt me

at midnight

i stay awake

thinking about

everything

we used to be

his confusion.

a man who sends you mixed signals

is a man who doesn't deserve you

the night is coming.

briefly

the sky a devilish red

the sun setting behind

the earth's face

i feel so alone

sitting next to you

my soul screams out

in silence

beneath the tension

consumed by darkness

bits of broken.

break my heart

and you'll find fragments

of all the love letters

i wrote to you

on each shattered piece

the failure.

i fail so often at love
that i choose seclusion
over the expectations
that come with being
in a relationship

certamine.

you struggle with love of self

and so when someone truly

adores your heart

you struggle with believing them

positionibus.

i'm always apologizing

when you hurt me

after assuming that i was trying

to hurt you, when i wasn't

no love near death.

there is death

in loving the wrong person

i sit and watch so many

of my peers die slow

sine sensu.

in love, alone

overrun with the desire

to feel nothing

suffering from the curse

of feeling everything

for someone

who feels nothing for you

12:53.

people who don't feel good

about themselves

arc always ready

to make others feel bad

about themselves

spem.

i hope you find someone

who never makes you feel bad

for being all that you are

the empty and blissful.

your apologies began to feel empty

"i'm sorry" triggered no emotion

to feel nothing for you

was everything i thought

it would be

peaceful in the absence

of your presence

empty union.

you not acknowledging
the love i showed you
will always be the worst part
of our union

always after midnight.

i'm left rereading old messages

sitting beneath the rubble

of everything we used to be

haunted, near the moon

by everything we didn't become

quaestio.

the only thing you were good at

was making me feel like i was the problem

in poetry.

tears become words

pain becomes strength

heartbreak becomes a testimony

of how i found myself

after losing you

me, you.

encounter me

and find the love

you deserve

untitled I.

stay close to the people
who remind your soul
to remain strong

Marie.

i want to live on the pages

of your heart

i want to find life

in the stories

that make you smile

you, your heart.

falling apart doesn't make you weak

a strong heart is capable of breaking

no solutions.

i wanted to try

i was willing to fight for this

you wanted a way out

you never cared as much as me

takes time sometimes.

every time you answer their call

or reply to their text

you have to restart the process

of moving

assist.

she doesn't always
have to save herself
the queen doesn't have to be
content with standing alone
being strong doesn't have
to feel lonely
it's okay to let someone take care of you
while you work on loving yourself

3:27.

the person who deserves your love

won't treat you poorly

love is not an excuse

to stay with someone

who can't love you correctly

no courage.

i could have been your everything

but you didn't have the courage

to love me in the way i needed

newfound.

sometimes i miss the anticipation

that attaches itself to new love

the longing and newfound desire

to learn everything about a beautiful stranger

all the tales we tell.

incapable of facing the painful reality

of a love that's been lost

we lie in the form of false memories

re-creating disaster and chaos

into beautiful moments

that never happened

after all, in the end.

oftentimes

tragedy transforms

into beauty

delightful things occur

in the aftermath of chaos

just be patient

to our seeds.

one day i may have daughters

and i don't want them to believe

that their independence is a burden

or restriction on love

no restriction.

your independence is not

some curse or restriction

your independence doesn't have

to be an excuse as to why you're single

you still deserve to be loved correctly

your independence should be celebrated

and supported while in a relationship

being independent doesn't make you unlovable

being independent doesn't mean

you always have to fight alone

independent women still deserve

the deepest love

and wanting to be loved

and cared for

doesn't have to compromise

a woman's strength and independence

7:14.

strong women only intimidate

the type of men that'll never

be able to comprehend

or understand their worth

all of her.

a body betrayed

a heart destroyed

a mind in confusion

and yet a woman

is capable of taking pain

and transforming it into triumph

healthy spirit.

more mental health

and a peace of mind

protect your right

to feel at ease

coffee and a book.

shades and shadows

the smell of coffee beans

sits in my nostrils

the taste of Colombia on my tongue

the pages of my favorite book

between my fingers

my morning bliss

has just begun

internet trolls.

i give silence to your criticism
as you've decided to exaggerate
your own importance to my art

i give silence to your opinions
because in my opinion
you are wrong

i give silence to your anger
because i'm happy and in love

i give silence to your opinion
while you remain below
i rise above

<u>sick day.</u>

give your soul a break

if you're tired of being hurt

just rest awhile

<u>not a victim, victor.</u>

hate me, i love it

get angry, i'll just laugh

March 17th I.

i got tired of practicing
the self-destruction
of fighting for someone
who would rather fight
against me

that's not love

<u>March 17th II.</u>

if you're in a relationship
with someone who
doesn't respect your mind and heart
it's time to move on
without that person

if you're in a relationship
that doesn't support your joy
and peace of mind
it's time to move forward
without that person

March 17th III.

feel what you feel but also understand

that most people don't deserve

an emotional reaction from you

you are valuable

you are grand

you are the essence of strength

don't let them break you

March 17th IV.

you're always trying
but who tries for you
you're always fighting
but who fights for you

i hate this idea of everything
falling upon the shoulders
of a woman
while she's in a relationship
with a man who makes no effort

i hate this idea of a woman
feeling alone while being
in a relationship

March 17th V.

i learned so many lessons in love
the hard way
i learned that loving someone
doesn't simply make them the one

i learned that love
in its purest form
can only be provided
and accepted when
you love yourself first

March 17th VI.

there is value in your presence

there is value within your heart

and not everyone can afford

to be with someone like you

that's fine

March 17th VII.

for me personally

i would not have found love

in someone else

until i found it in its

purest form within myself first

you are the beginning

it all starts with you

the love you long for

must first be cultivated on your own

by yourself

March 17th VIII.

i think what we've found in dating
is that sometimes
the people we care for are incapable
of caring for us the way we need

we discover through relationships
that sometimes the person
we fall for cannot comprehend
the love we provide

March 17th IX.

having standards is not a burden

being strong is not a burden

the mate you choose

should always choose you

just you

March 17th X.

the love you accept

shouldn't hurt you

the relationship you entertain

shouldn't cause confusion

a terrible terror of love II.

it's scary how dedicated

you can be to someone

who would rather use their energy

to attempt to destroy you

cost of communication.

know your worth

and never communicate

reply or respond to anyone

who can't afford to speak to you

or with you

she, you, woman.

delicate yet strong
there's a certain balance
that only a woman like her
can obtain

she knows what she deserves
and provided anything less
she'll walk away in search of more

she's guarded, sure
but she's ready to open up
to the one who deserves her

6:42.

you've been hurt

you've made your mistakes

you've been called out

of your name

you've felt broken

you've fallen down

you've had to pick up the pieces

of your heart and start over

you've been mishandled, neglected

disrespected and you've felt unprotected

all of which has caused you to guard your heart
but you're stronger

look at what you've been through

you're a queen who always gets through

you're a woman who continues to survive

it's evident.

something within you
is hurting, you're in pain
and it shows in the songs
you relate to
the quotes and poetry
you double-tap on social media
and of course it's evident
from the way these words make you feel
but things do change, as you know
things do get better and they will

6:53.

so many things i need to work on

so many fucking things i need to change

false claims of real love.

i find that it's difficult

to find a heart that wants

to love you permanently

so many "i love yous"

from people who don't

intend to stay

7:05.

don't let the pain
of any past relationship
prevent you from finding
something genuine and real
in the future of something new

weak critique.

i've come to realize that

negative criticism

often arrives from the lips

of someone incapable of accomplishing

the things you can

the roses.

she is a storm of roses

dangerous but beautiful

8:32.

too often the heart

finds a way to love

the ones who will never

love it back

broken chains.

loving myself more
set me free of you

daydreaming life.

my life rarely fits
the picture i draw up
in my head

having certain expectations
has ruined me

the levels.

there are several levels to love

don't be afraid to reach

for the highest

a short moment.

the truth hurts

and so we find peace

in lies that create

a temporary happiness

the never-ending never.

hating kills progression

i know this because

all the people who hate me

will surely never surpass me

8:49.

my ego and my soul

have found the perfect compromise

a void.

i felt like a bookstore

with no books on its shelves

a profound emptiness

in my soul

demands never met.

somehow i'd always feel
a deep regret when asking for more
knowing damn well
that having any sort of expectation
would ruin me in ways
that i could never imagine

while my requests were met
with nothing or lack of effort
i was simply demanding everything
i knew i deserved
everything you weren't willing to give
and i know that now

knowing you.

who are you when no one is watching
can i trust that person to remain loyal
without my watchful eyes

who are you when my back is turned
can i trust that person to be honest
in my absence

i see a lifetime in brown eyes.

the morning comes too soon
your eyes a weary shade of brown
your hair twisted and tangled
restless and yet you smile

the sun rises on your face
shining brighter than before
you lean in to whisper "i love you"
but in this moment, i love you more

March 23rd.

i've become a flower and rose

enthusiast because i've fallen in love

i've come to the realization that loving

a woman

means making an effort to make her smile

at all times

why give her grief and sorrow

when you can give her roses

that scream "i love you"

24 hours.

i do whatever i can
to protect my partner's peace of mind
when you love someone
you keep that relationship secure and safe
love shouldn't feel like chaos and hell

a truth I.

holding on to someone
who doesn't care about losing you
causes you to lose yourself
and self-esteem

i witnessed.

watching you decide

to miss out on real love

because you'd rather hold on

to someone who doesn't love you

is the hardest part

a truth II.

your opinion of me
will never define who i truly am
and whatever you think of me
holds no importance in my life

surviving oceans.

we're drowning for people

who refuse to pull us from an ocean

of despair

we're drowning for people

who tipped us over

forcing us to be submerged

by our own pain

we're drowning as they watch

without a care in this world

we're drowning and only we

can save ourselves

mature men.

having many women means nothing
being able to juggle several women
doesn't make you a man
but the strength and determination
to love and be faithful to one does

further from truth.

amazing isn't it

the way that every lie that gets told

contains just enough truth to seem believable

but not enough truth to be true

a truth III.

the woman who asks for more

isn't asking for too much

the woman who demands more

is simply in search of everything

she deserves

a truth IV.

and that's the issue

sometimes when you see what you want

you forget what you need

and what you accept is further

from what you deserve

noncombative.

the beauty in being secure with self

is that you never have to defend your ideas

or your actions

with people who don't matter

ability.

she has the patience to stay
and the strength to move on

valued.

when a man realizes the value

of the woman who shares herself with him

he adds value to himself

uncontrollable.

seek the approval of no one

never change who you are

to fit the mold that others

have created for you

imitation.

some apologize

because they mean it

others apologize

because they've gotten caught

withdrawn but progressive.

i'm constantly evolving
i just wish you were involved
and a part of this change

i've been doing this without you
but i'm fine

beneath above.

she desires a patient partner

one who will dig deeper

making sure she reaches

her peak

lower.

understand that a woman's love

is something that runs deep

if you're not ready and willing

to reach her depths

don't attempt the dive

don't waste her time

inner, deeper.

when i hear the word "woman"
so many things come to mind
my thoughts are overtaken
by great things and visions

i value the essence, mind
and the very being of a woman

see, many men look at a woman
and categorize her by the way she looks
reducing her to her appearance
but i see more than that

i'm willing to go to the depths
of the soul, the mind
its core

the most beautiful woman is far more
than a beautiful structure or what
she appears to be to the naked eye

the most beautiful woman has gold
running through her veins and magic
living within her heart

you are that woman . . .

sex, poetry in motion.

let us lie

beside

beneath

one another

using our emotions to convey

express

and act out the actions of our mind

body

soul

and heart

sex is poetry in motion

with a touch of love

adding meaning to what

is already beautiful

you and i

beneath the moon

covered in darkness

let us create

let us write

when together.

touch her in a way that no one
has done before
stimulate her entire mind
with an abundance of words
and leave an imprint upon her soul

create a long-lasting memory
and become something she'll
never forget
a lasting impression is what
you should always aim for

appreciate all that she is
and all that she's willing to offer

it's what she deserves

11:59.

she knew what she had to do

and as the clock counted down

the new year would stare her

right in the face

urging and pleading for her

to make the necessary changes

to bring forth the love

she desired and deserved

12:00.

but that's the thing

the most honest and hurtful truth

i don't think they changed

they simply became more

of who they always were

and the person you see now

is the type of person

you've tried your hardest

to avoid but it's hard to let go

because you've already fallen for them

12:07.

you've been holding on
to someone who no longer
deserves your grip
you've lost countless hours of sleep
thinking about someone who doesn't
deserve to be on your mind

you've displayed an amazing ability
to care so deeply unconditionally
and you're beautiful because of that

one day you'll be rewarded
with a love that mirrors your own
but first you must move on
without the person who refuses
to love you

12:21.

i can't stay here
i'm tired of being tired
i'm exhausted from yelling
and not being heard

i no longer wish to fight with
someone who refuses to fight for me
i am no longer willing
to wear this coat of unhappiness
i miss my smile and i'll only find it
with you gone
but instead of asking you
to go
i'll leave

killing the cycle.

not again

never, not anymore

i can't

i won't

i'm done

i'm gone

12:29.

lately

you haven't been yourself

your laughter isn't as loud

your smile appears to be forced

and i just think you'd do well

with focusing more on yourself

for a while

you, royal.

today, just like any other day
you'll rise from the ashes
a fire set by those who wish
for you to fail
and the prayer in your heart
will remain stronger
than the words of your enemies

you are mighty
and your strength
is your crown

broken nightmare.

you refused to live
within the nightmare
sold to you as a dream

you finally woke up

sharp.

open your damn eyes

your suspicion can be justified

by their actions as of late

don't second-guess your heart

you know the truth

to the root.

and they wonder why
you have trust issues
or act as if you don't
give a fuck

the way you are
the way you love
is a product
of being taken
for granted

August 29th.

some relationships

are just hurtful distractions

keeping you from the love

you long for

12:50.

be with me
and only me
choose me always
because i'll always
choose you

much for nothing.

she poured her heart out to me
on pages i refused to read
texting me every night
"you are all that i need"
blinded by a situation
blurring my ability to see
she screamed
"i know that this means nothing
but you mean everything to me"

so consistent were her efforts
she was willing to wait
she said
"you think you love this girl
but you're my soul mate"

her heart cries in need of me
but her smile is all they see
it meant everything to her
but never meant much to me

hoarding of the past.

my home is overflowing

with things i'll never need

no space for anything new

because i'm holding on to things

from my past that have no value

in the present

in the ashes of.

burn bridges for warmth

burn bridges for light

burn bridges to others

who don't deserve

to get to you

1:21.

i am cold

i am warmth

i am numb

i feel everything

i am all but nothing

i give love and i hate it

Plath.

reading Sylvia's words

wishing i could save her

wishing i could tell her

that it will get better

stillness.

you speak

in silence

so well

finis.

it all falls on me

the weight of it all

crushing my spirit

like bone meeting iron

i'm breaking down

collapsing completely into

myself

until there's nothing left

but the regret

of trying so hard

for someone who couldn't

try for me

i'm done

the wrong, the negative.

the right people help you feel

the right things

the wrong people encourage

all of the emotions

you don't want to feel

stay away from the wrong people

belief in the process.

learning to detach from things
that serve no purpose in my life

busy.

being busy keeps the soul happy

doing nothing makes you feel

like nothing

transformations.

they chose to be sheep

she decided to be a wolf

<u>deeply mad.</u>

love me madly

like crazy is the new sane

i feel both entirely.

i am both happy and sad

i feel weak but i am strong

i am broken but i'll be whole

there is hope within pain

there is hope after heartache

and i've felt both of everything

i know that it gets better

book of souls.

read her like books
that intrigue the soul

careful as i choose.

i'm careful about the people
i choose to entertain
because attention can become love
and love can feel like hell
when given to the wrong person

you live in these words.

come

see yourself in these words

come alive within my poetry

find clarity and peace

within the pages of this book

allow my art to touch your soul

allow these words to grasp your heart

child of the moon.

you are a living extension

of the moon in the night

a light that shines the brightest

during the darkness

the hurting of self.

you've been chasing

all the ones who will never

love you

distracting yourself

from the one

who deserves that love

in gardens we wait.

each of us, roses

waiting to be picked

chosen by the hand

who isn't afraid of our thorns

searching the emptiness.

isn't that how it always begins
attraction sparked by the surface
something pleasing for the eye
something hopeful for the heart

here you are spending your days
and nights
in search of someone
to take the pain away
but what you discover
is someone who creates more pain

for the culture.

someone tagged me in a photo

with my words on their skin

i lost a lot of friends on this journey

but something like that feels like a win

more aqua.

drink more water
and stay away from people
with negative attitudes
and petty behavior

maintaining peace I.

being with someone who refuses

to protect your heart

will distract you from the things

that would otherwise make you happy

the saddest part of it all

is that we'll claim to want peace

and yet we'll settle for

a chaotic relationship

then complain about it

maintaining peace II.

the worst kinds of people

are those who are unhappy

with your need to experience happiness

detach from these types of people

a table for one.

your words are no longer yours

your voice the tone of someone else's

you've changed who you are

for validation and profit

still, you've discovered

that success only arrives

to those who remain authentic

and this is why you

continue to lose

overdone, exhausting.

trying until trying

is something that i'll no longer do

loving you until

i realize that it'll change nothing

these things take time

and i'm patient

a refusal, a strength.

i'm finding more of myself
in my journey toward peace
learning to let go of the anger
that once plagued my soul
and altered the direction
of most of my days

i'm finding my voice
beneath the heaviness
of the pain that once caused me
to shut down
refusing to remain silent
about the things that broke me
i refuse to be a prisoner of heartache

afraid, my silence.

we lie to ourselves

we hide behind our own masks

we suppress our truths

with tall drinks and loud music

self-medicating with sex

self-harming with acts of recklessness

we'd rather pretend to be happy

instead of cultivating long-term happiness

smiling to cover up the emotional bruises

left upon our soul by lovers

who never loved us

giving off the appearance of strength

while breaking down deep within

and yet no one ever knows

because being strong often means

being silent

i hate that i allowed my voice

to be silenced by my inability

to ask for help

i hate that i allowed this pain

to consume me in a way

that no one will truly know about

afraid to admit to myself that i cared

because accepting the truth

would reveal the hurt that found

its way into my heart

4:00.

up early

while the world

is still dreaming

it's 4 a.m.

and the city that never sleeps

is sleeping as this is written

wide wake

lying beside my dream girl

proving once more

that dreams come true

and you don't have to be asleep

to bear witness to it all

:22 after 4.

22 minutes after 4

my soul at peace

my mind, widely aware

my heart pumping

giving me life

and a purpose to write

yesterday is yesterday

irrelevant, most unworthy

of this moment

the present being a gift

only given to those who open

their eyes

i am here among the living

and even if life is hard

it's beautiful because i'm alive

it's worth it, you wait and see

4:32.

the unfortunate truth
of going to bed angry
is that you wake up weary
drained by the sadness that follows
and it swallows you up
with whatever good you had left

you wake up tired
longing for peace
but it easily escapes you
because in that moment
you're too tired to pursue it

change the way you go to sleep
and you'll wake up better
stronger, wiser

clarity in mourning.

i tried

you didn't

i loved

you refused

it was me

and never you

it was you

not wanting me

stuck, searching for you

when all i needed was myself

the love you deserve.

they want you

but none of them

deserve you

they like you

but none of them

will love you

take your time

and find more of yourself

before searching for more

of someone else

the love you desire

needs to be cultivated

within you first

before you can find it elsewhere

the optimism and delight.

a different you

sitting in a brighter hue

gone are the days of darkness

gone, the days of sadness

a smile that bears light

like the sun rising against the ocean

a laughter that bears life

like a tree standing in the forest

this is my hope for you

and i know you'll find it someday

when night falls.

good mornings
can replace bad nights
never underestimate
the sun burning out
the darkness

create more.

don't let your past corrupt

the present

don't let the painful memories

you've created

keep you from the creation

of something better

from it, stronger.

the pain will bring you strength
the heartache will give you purpose

more you, mighty.

somehow the sorrow

made you this

wise

stronger

beautiful

more of you

pursuing nothing.

the wrong love

feels like death

and i felt myself

slipping away

while chasing after you

with the absence of you.

apparently i never needed you

i know this now

as i found everything i wanted

without you here

you, a delight.

you are an unforgettable moment
a lifetime of delight
don't let them fool you into thinking
that your presence means nothing
don't let them fool you into thinking
that somehow you're ordinary

Dahlia.

i haven't spoken to my mother

in such a long time

so long, that pieces of me

have begun to fade

into everything we used to be

and everything i used to feel

becomes lost with time

too long, the distance.

it takes us too long

to figure out that love

doesn't have to hurt

and the love we give

is too precious to be given away

to someone who refuses

to give it back

remember before.

who were you

before sadness overran your heart

i hope you remember

what it felt like to be happy

on your own, within.

find your calm

reclaim your peace

re-create the love

you couldn't find in others

become it.

the only one worthy of you

is you

in this moment

you only need yourself

become the love

that they refused to share with you

be loud, no silence.

find your strength

find the courage

reclaim your voice

and say what you need

to say

do not be silent

be loud

be unapologetic

be entirely you

without regret

distancing a memory.

every day since we ended

i've developed new ways

to push you further

from my memory

i want you out

of my mind

as i recall.

a strong memory

is the destroyer

of the heart

starlit.

count the stars

that live within yourself

you're brighter than you know

:09.

loving you drained my spirit

:11.

do it

on your own

do it

for yourself

do it

at your own pace

:14.

i know too much
and say too little
while screaming
on the inside

fin, love.

we ended

i was never yours

to have, to hold

to keep

mind, the enemy.

i struggled to forget

but you've forgotten me already

read, lover.

books stained with the tears

of the reader with the broken heart

books held tight

like lovers in the dark

sometimes all you have are the words

sometimes all that's left

are the books

text ignored, no response I.

please
text me back

are you
still mad

say something
if not anything else

tell me what to do

i'll do better
i can be better

help me understand
can i have another chance

submerged, fighting.

i'm here

in the deep end

struggling to save myself

while you watch me drown

text ignored, no response II.

please don't leave me
i get it now, i understand

i still need you

we were happy
i don't know what changed

are you there
are you listening
don't shut me out

fade into shadows.

we were happy once

the sun shined its light

on us, together

but the love faded

into the shadows of the sunset

and here we are

filled with nothing

showing shades of emptiness

a void no longer filled

with love and respect

strangers again, again.

we started as strangers
we ended that way
sometimes the beginning
is the same as the ending

my response I.

fuck the writers

who write irrelevant things

about me

because they're incapable

of writing anything as relevant

as what i've written

my response II.

fuck the writers

who gang up to accuse

or abuse the authors

who achieve more than

they ever will

or ever thought possible

my response III.

may your hatred become a shovel

that digs your own grave

my hope is that you rest in peace

with the hateful words you spewed

directly or indirectly

these words, this book

in memory of all the people

who dislike me

or others like me

a funeral held for those

who will soon be forgotten

buried beneath my words

buried beneath my success

no longer.

after begging for a truth
that has been kept from you
emotional exhaustion sets in
you've been strong but now
you're tired of being lied to
you're tired of being denied
the respect that you've fought for
while fighting for a space in their life

the begging and pleading
is replaced with the silence of anger
the silence of resentment
the silence that seems the loudest
as your refusal to speak
screams of your disappointment
and your newfound commitment
to yourself

a silent declaration of the desire

to now detach your heart

from the heart that hurts you

after demanding the truth for so long

you've reached your breaking point

untold tale.

sometimes i wish

i could take my secrets back

i hate the fact that you know me

in ways you didn't deserve

aching.

it hurts
the pain of feeling nothing
the realization that being numb
is best

it hurts because
i'd like to feel again
but i'm afraid of feeling for
the wrong person

a quiet expression.

the silence tells me everything

a wordless expression

a quiet resentment and regret

you can almost hear everything

that isn't being said

a nonexistent us.

i am becoming less afraid

of a reality that isn't centered around us

i am becoming more accepting

of a life lived without you

blurred self.

all of this

all of that

all of me

but it was

never enough

the pursuit of you

destroyed my self-esteem

a teen spirit.

i want to slow dance to Nirvana

with you, love

agonize.

we search for something
to take the pain away
but what we find is someone
who causes more pain

a wishing well.

i really wish you well

i hope things get better for you

i hope you change your ways

i don't wish the pain you caused me

on anyone else

and so i hope your heart learns

to feel love in its purest form

because if it doesn't

you'll miss out on something real

just as you missed out on being

with me

<u>potion.</u>

she refused to be anyone's cup of tea

she was more so the finest glass of whiskey

vex.

it's fucked up

because the people

who break you

are always okay

while you're in pain

discern, you.

your smile breaks my heart

because it's not real

and as much as i care

there's nothing i can do

to help but give you these words

in hopes of letting you know

that you're not alone

i see you . . .

comrade.

you are your own best friend

don't abandon yourself

become everything you need

retain.

so many men know

what it takes to make

a woman fall in love

but most of them

can't comprehend what it takes

to keep a woman in love

not adequate.

you were only good

at pretending to be

what i wanted

but you were never

good enough for me

looking glass.

sometimes everything you're looking for
hides within your own reflection

it's time to start looking for you
it's time to start looking for yourself

tussle.

i know you can do this
if you can't be strong
be brave, keep fighting

a sturdy heart.

and if on this day
all you did was smile
even while you wanted
to break down

be proud of yourself
for standing
while wanting to fall

factual.

a man who loves you

will not force you to compromise

your emotional well-being

or the health of your heart

campaign.

women are warriors
without physical weapons
the way they use their minds
to conquer whatever attempts
to break them

March 25th.

it'll happen

you'll either entertain

or fall for someone

who made you feel as if

they were the one

it happens often

you meet a person

you get to know them

feelings begin to surge throughout your heart

and you start to imagine

a future with that person

it happens to the best of us

things begin to change

that feeling of security

begins to fade

as that relationship goes on

you find yourself fighting

to stay afloat on a boat

that is slowly sinking

you plug those holes with denial

you plug those holes with lies

telling yourself it's okay

you make excuses

for the way that person treats you

you start to lose yourself

because you're more concerned

with keeping a person that appears

to no longer care about keeping you

March 26th.

when you go back to someone

who mistreated you

you're cheating yourself

out of an opportunity

to be with someone

who will always consider your feelings

her silence, a sign.

sometimes a woman's silence

serves as proof that she no longer

gives a fuck

and you're no longer worth

her energy

more, most.

you deserve the deepest

most sincere form of pleasure

December 27th.

i'm beginning to wake up

love is blind at times

but time also has a way

of waking us up to the bullshit

that often attaches itself

to loving someone who can't provide

the same level of love

we express

we often settle

failing to realize

that there exists someone

capable of reflecting

the same level of love

we give them

January 1st.

loving the wrong person

provides a lesson

in what to look for

as far as warning signs

within your future relationships

January 1st, 8:55 p.m.

it's amazingly sad
when someone fails to understand
how much you truly care for them
but you can't hold on to that pain

one day they'll look back
with so many regrets
and you'll be with the one
who loves you back
you'll be with someone
who would fight to keep you

January 4th, 5:43 p.m.

my heart is open once more
after being closed
while with someone
who promised to keep it safe

time alters what's familiar
people change
you never see it coming

hesitant to love again
but again my heart is open
you've felt what i felt
so let us fall together
and i'll help you fix
what he has broken

January 7th, 8:49 p.m.

before i get the chance
to place my hands on your skin
i'd first like the opportunity
for our souls to collide
our minds to be fully stimulated
and our hearts to be in sync

this is the way i'd like to love you

January 7th, 8:26 a.m.

on this morning
i feel at ease
the stress has gone
i can't truly explain what i feel
at this very moment
but it's a feeling that has escaped me
for far too long

i'm okay
on a path to being happy again

8:39:52 p.m.

i'd love every part of you

if you allowed it

inside and out

5:27:15 p.m.

and the silence is all you have

to offer to those

you no longer give a fuck about

4:23:08 p.m.

what i desire more than anything

is a relationship with someone

who doesn't mind the idea

of spending a lifetime with one person

7:52:20 p.m.

i couldn't help myself
before i knew it
my hands were on her thigh
her skirt beginning to rise
with no desire to rush
i inched my fingers
a bit closer to her flower
as i preferred the act
to unfold organically

i then touched her in a way
that caused a weakness
within her spine
ever so apparent by the way
she lay down on my mattress
like rain, falling from a cloud

"it's been a while," she whispered
as i proceeded to take her

January 10th.

this craving to explore

the unfamiliar places within you

has overtaken my mind

i'd like to get lost in you

i'd like the opportunity

to make you feel things

you've never felt for anyone else

9:29:13 a.m.

i woke up with the taste of her
still lingering on my tongue
erotic visuals burned into my mind
her skin slightly wet
from the activity we engaged in

"it's yours," she whispered
muffled moans became screams
as i explored the deepest parts
of her existence

9:29:38 p.m.

i'm addicted to this idea

of your legs wrapped around

my waist

holding me in place

as if to say

you'll never let me go

wet walls.

can we pause for a second

and thank the heavens for angels

with strong wings

and soft skin

inner thighs like pillows

legs that bow like oval shapes

wrapped around my face

like blindfolds made of silk

i stopped wishing for moments like this
the very moment you allowed me

to live it

completely, explicitly

your openness as wide as your spread eagle

your wet walls

like the insides of our mouths

warm and waiting

i've been anticipating you just as much

as you've been wanting me

6:16 p.m.

utilizing my tongue

as a stress reliever

pressing pressure points

creating a climax

provoking pleasure

with ease

opening you right up

because my tongue

is the key

guide me.

i'd like to get lost in you

mind, body, and soul

travel the avenues that lead me

to a greater understanding of you

show me your fears, the horror

the pain, the struggle

reveal your thoughts

as you overthink

show me the flaws

you try your hardest to hide

the sadness that sits beneath your smile

i'd like to know the real you

the you that you're afraid

to show the world

the girl behind the shade

of a fake smile

i want to see the things

that you think will chase me away

i'd like to understand

and later learn to love you

for who you truly are

profess, encourage.

teach the many possibilities
to a child
never make a child feel like
their dreams are impossible
to achieve

a healing.

when i open the book
i turn off the pain

the reader.

the girls who love books

have the sweetest love to give

a rare find, love.

give me something

that can't easily be found

help me rediscover

new reasons to smile

the carving of.

you've written your initials

on my soul

your love, carved into me

let us begin, love.

i want you wildly
and recklessly

i want you here
right next to me

i want the adventure
in your heart

so take my hand
and we can start

wanting, afraid.

you are everything i want

you are everything i'm afraid of

this craving for love

met with the fear of getting hurt

but i'll risk it all

for a moment on your mind

and a place in your heart

7:22:22 p.m.

i see love in those brown eyes

i see warmth in your embrace

i feel a forever whenever i'm with you

memory museum.

i relive all of the moments

we've shared

and all of the memories we've created

every time my lips touch yours

the broken meet the broken.

a love between two broken people

can feel whole and complete

maybe we're puzzles

and you were holding the piece

i needed the entire time

i just had to find you first

scary in the beginning

as your pain matched my own

both hurt and burned by love

we met one another

we held one another

then fell for one another

both of our scars visible

and yet the vision of us together

still remained beautiful

feeling, hiding.

you ever get so sad
that you laugh
you ever feel so hurt
that you smile

we're so good at hiding
behind what we wish to feel
we're so good at pretending
to feel nothing
when we feel everything

behind hate, behind pain.

i finally realized

that love hides itself

behind the people who hurt us

meaning,

you have to look beyond the pain

to find the love you deserve

it's always there

you just have to stop letting

certain people distract you from it

no shame on the broken.

broken people need to understand

that being hurt is nothing to be ashamed of

and just because you're broken

doesn't mean you'll never find a pure love

aware, mindful.

depression has eaten its way

to my heart

there's a sadness that lingers there

my mind overrun by painful thoughts

sometimes i hate being this aware

harsh lessons.

the one person

who was supposed to help me

fix this shit

was the first person

to leave when i needed them the most

this was one of the harshest lessons

i'd ever learn

sometimes the only person

you need is yourself

the mental freedom.

thinking about you
sucked me further
into darkness

and as hard as it's been
i've been working harder
to free my mind of you

the slow burning of regret.

i hope the memory of me
burns through your mind
and in times of desperation
i hope you reach for me
then realize that i can no longer
be found

you'll feel what i felt
you'll sit with your face
in your hands
and your heart on the floor
because you lost the greatest thing
to ever happen to you
me . . .

silent night.

sometimes you just need

to be alone with yourself

and the silence of solitude

in order to figure everything out

a stillness.

be still and conquer

again, all over.

if i could do it all again
i would've loved me more
instead of waiting on you

all of me.

my personality is a secret

and i can only share it with you

once you've earned my trust

small and great.

so much power

in one little woman

the anti.

no tolerance for drama

no room for fake individuals

i keep to myself

because i prefer peace

books, therapeutic.

she sat in the corner

with her face in a book

hiding from anxiety

trying not to panic

connect to.

while others were searching

for wi-fi

i was searching

for a soul connection

she, in wonderland.

where do you go

when you daydream

wherever it is

i imagine

that you're happy there

smiling into the distance

beautiful while getting lost

steel curtain.

protect your energy

understand that not everyone

who wants you

deserves you

protect your peace of mind

understand that most people

don't even deserve to be a thought

introvert I.

i am more myself

when i am alone

empty, emptier.

empty people

filling themselves

with people

who fill them up

with more emptiness

more sadness

more pain

it lives there.

silence is a home

and it houses everything

i'll never say

introvert II.

sometimes i don't want to be

around too many people

sometimes i just don't feel like talking

sometimes i dread

human interaction

and i'm not ashamed of that

sometimes, the silence.

silence for those

who either aren't ready

to listen

or don't deserve

to hear your thoughts

oh, shy soul.

the most intriguing soul

belongs to the shy human

introvert III.

in silence

i listen

i observe

i see all

i know all

i understand

and can't be fooled

the trying.

watching all the people

trying to fit happiness

into shopping bags

noses buried in liquor

trying to forget

drowning out the pain

with loud music

trying their hardest

to be content with being hurt

from heartache.

let pain inspire
your power

let heartache
inspire your heart
to grow stronger

introvert IV.

i am rarely alone

when by myself

i am more alone

with others

staying in tonight.

say "no" more often

tell them you're just not interested

no more doing things

that you have no desire to do

for the sake of other people's feelings

the introversion.

people are draining

i find fullness in being alone

outgoing, introvert.

she, a chameleon
capable of fitting in
but made to stand out

an outgoing introvert
if something like that could exist
but even in a sea of people
she still felt alone

don't talk to me.

a phone or a book

some headphones might do

all of these things

which prevent me

from having to talk to people

all of these things

to help me appear

uninterested

<u>spring.</u>

break me open

and roses will grow

between the cracks

k–12.

i'm tired
of being tired
of being around
people

start here, with self.

real love arrives

when we're ready

real love arrives

when we love ourselves

hell in mind.

we carry around hell

in the form of memories

moments shared with people

who no longer mean anything

to our lives

more substance, more life.

i'd go out and party

then come home to the moon

an empty home

and cold bed

this was no way to live

i needed more

one-sided vow.

being married

doesn't save a marriage

loving someone

doesn't make them

your soul mate

trying harder

doesn't mean

they'll try just as much

going to therapy

won't help a person

who doesn't think

they need to change

your denial

is your own

personal prison

all talk without action.

he'd say anything

to make her stay

but never did enough

to keep her from leaving

jealousy, all-consuming.

you see

they want you

to do well

just not better than them

the support begins to fade

the more successful you become

heart filled with envy

jealousy consumes their souls

fake family and friends

and you'll have to let them go

never anything more.

you were never

what i needed

you never became

the person

you promised to be

no end.

a happy ending is not enough

i deserve

i require

i demand a happiness

that doesn't have to end

reality says.

we do too much

for those who don't do enough

we give our all

to those

who do nothing

we're searching for peace

in relationships

overrun with hatred

over all else.

i care more about

my own happiness

than the hatred

that people feel for me

i am a priority

within my own life

i choose me

every time

arm raised.

most of my critics

are only critical of me

because i continue

to move beyond

the limitations

they've set on my craft

and most of the hate

i've received from other writers

is derived from

their inability to achieve

what i've achieved

i am totally accepting

of their defeat

i am completely content

with winning

above the rest.

when you insult my words
you insult my readers

but insulting my art, me
and my supporters
does nothing but keep you
stranded beneath us

royal.

Samantha King
queen of my future
a ruler on her own
a warrior
through and through

a painful thought.

it's the memories
the painful ones

what we remember
poisons the heart

higher up.

you belong to the night

next to the brightest stars

in sync with the moon

above the earth

your own reflection.

i was a mirror

in our relationship

and maybe you left

because you didn't like

what you saw

a beautiful mess.

i traveled to the messiest

parts of her mind

and found beauty there

forever summer.

you make winters feel hot
i'm in desperate need
of your warmth

sad melodies.

you helped me relate

to the saddest of songs

my heart ran blue

because of you

introverted war.

it's like i want to be alone

but i want to be touched

in daydreams.

she lives inside of her head
to escape the reality
surrounding her

never felt like home.

home is where the heart
can feel secure and safe

i was homeless
when loving you

for love, for you.

but i'd drain the entire ocean

to keep you from drowning

an empty love.

you said enough

to make me believe

but never enough

to keep me from leaving

foolish denial.

i let you break me
then waited for you
to fix me

6:05 a.m.

it happens
you know

sometimes
broken people
break others

you were allowed.

what truly hurts
is that i was happier
before you arrived

and letting you in
was like inviting chaos
into my life
allowing you
to invade my peace

all for love, irony.

isn't it ironic

how the need for love

draws us closer to hate

the love you desire.

the best kind of love
is the one that never ends
it's there whenever you need it
it holds on without letting go

lights.

you need only to be with someone

who brings out the light in you

be.

be who you are
stand tall in what you believe

accept yourself
don't wait for the world
to love you

love is many things.

another person's sexual orientation

has nothing to do with you

and your criticism of who

they choose to love

is unimportant and irrelevant

love, your way.

do not hide your love
behind the hatred of others

do not allow others
to dictate who
or how you love

deep heaven.

kiss the hell out of the one
who helps you find heaven
on earth

be loud.

if women
were silent
the world
would lose
its voice

if women
held back
the world
would lose
its strength

6:31:05 a.m.

the supporting of women

the encouraging of women

the motivation of women

doesn't in any way

equate to hating men

6:34:30 a.m.

just because
you are kind to her
doesn't mean
she owes you sex

6:37:10 a.m.

do not trade in your strength

to make him feel stronger

do not exchange your voice

for his comfort

everything is everything.

i will always be too much

of everything

for someone who is incapable

of being everything to me

yours truly.

your beauty is yours

your body is yours

you are yours

you don't exist for them

a danger.

sadly

the biggest danger to us all

are the people we trust

they have the keys

to violate us in the worst of ways

you're not worthy.

disliking you as much

as you hate me

would require

an emotional commitment

that you don't deserve

moving on, self-love.

it ended
because i realized
that you didn't love me
like i love me

none.

no tolerance for

racism

sexism

and homophobia

zero tolerance

for anyone

who thrives upon hatred

8:29:10 a.m.

without a doubt
i can
and i will
free myself

below busy feet.

the busy have no time

to respond to the criticism

from those hating below them

<u>Aries.</u>

the goal is to avoid boredom

and never grow content with being lazy

or doing nothing

the mundane.

i seem to attract hatred

and criticism

from people who are content

with achieving less than me

i find that these individuals

travel in packs, fueled by hatred

or their inability to accomplish

the things that the people they hate on

have done

they're always so mundane
and boring with their lackluster
and unoriginal insults

screaming loud but their voices
muffled under their ignorance
stretching out their bitter, short arms
toward people like me
yet i remain out of reach
almost untouchable
and they'll always be laughable
to say the least

more reading, more peace.

i've gone mad

and the library

is my asylum

my peace of mind

my heaven on earth

from voices, we evolve.

speak, woman

tell me everything

tell the world

do not be silent

yell if you need to

i want to listen

i want to learn from you

i want to evolve

based upon your wisdom

you inspire a difference

come, speak

change the world

everyone and their opinions.

do not allow the path

of your life

to be altered by people

who have no path

to follow

painful conclusion.

no one is hurting more
than the people
who are silent about the pain
that lives within their souls

why i write.

i write poetry

because it's much easier

to write it down

than to say it out loud

without breaking down

lying in the mirror.

you can lie to others

sometimes successfully

but you can't tell a lie

to yourself successfully

because no matter what you do

every night before you fall asleep

the truth will look you in the eye

and burn a hole within your mind

inspired self.

be inspired

by the pain you feel

and your heart's ability

to keep fighting

you are powerful

mighty beyond measure

she, godly.

she could calm the ocean
with a glance
she could quiet a storm
with a whisper

all-powerful
all-beautiful and all-knowing

she's a woman
and that made her
some sort of god

broken, a healing process.

being broken is the beginning

it's the process of rediscovering

what it means to feel whole once more

some of you may believe

that getting hurt is the end

but the pain that you experience

gives way to a path that may lead

to something more beautiful

or stronger than what you've had

it's okay to feel hurt

there's nothing wrong

with feeling broken

the pain is never easy

but never be ashamed

to feel whatever it is you feel

do not think less of yourself

because of someone's inability

to do more or give you more

of what you deserve

our ending, new beginnings.

i'll be the one

you couldn't keep

i'll be the memory

that hurts the most

i'll be the greatest loss

in your life

i'll be the one

you'll never be able

to come back to

all because i love me more

than you ever could

someone, searching for you.

you don't know it yet

but there is love lurking

around the corner

there is something truly beautiful

waiting for you in the distance

you don't know it yet

but there is someone

searching for someone

with a love like yours

there is someone

searching for someone

who can love them

the way you do

it gets better, hold on.

three years ago

i wrote myself a note

i wrote a letter to others

as well

detailing the pain

and suffering that lived

within my soul

three years ago

in that letter, the note

i wrote down from my heart

my mind, my wretched soul

detailing what was next

a desire to take my last breaths

three years ago

i wanted to die

three years later

i feel so fucking alive

:38 after.

away i go
conflicted
broken like glass
for a love
that wasn't real

no space.

you see

this is what i get

trying to force my love

in places

where it was never meant

to fit

OCD I.

i understand
no judgment here
we all need to be
in control of something

you don't have to be ashamed
you don't need to hide this from me

OCD II.

your ability

to be orderly

is not some disease

your desire

to maintain control

is not some disease

your rituals

are simply several attempts

to get it right

your desire

to achieve order

is not a disorder

a beautiful composition.

i wanted to tell you

that the OCD is not a curse

it's just a gift that the world

doesn't understand

i wanted to tell you

that the anxiety you feel

is just proof of your ability

to feel deeper levels of emotion

that others may not be able

to comprehend

i wanted to tell you

that the depression you experience

causes you to view the world

from a perspective that goes

beyond the surface

a surface that so many minds

can't handle

and that in itself makes you rare

and mighty, you're strong

the world says you're broken

but that just means you're beautiful to me

untitled II.

you are beautiful

you are powerful

you are rare

you are grand

you are majestic

your broken

is a gift

the pain

will make you

stronger

keep fighting

continue to survive

i'll fight beside you

April 1st.

she doesn't have to look good
for you
wear makeup for you
be thin for you
cook and clean for you

she is not for you
she doesn't belong to you

a true form of love.

real love isn't something
you force
real love is not something
you compete for
real love will never have you
compromise your peace and joy

April 2nd I.

demand the love you deserve

and be willing to walk away

from anyone who refuses

to reciprocate the love

you provide

April 2nd II.

no woman should feel like

she has to try harder for someone

who isn't trying for her

April 2nd III.

it's not your fault

you were never the problem

you can't be everything

to someone

who deserves nothing

from you

i now know.

you could never be
what i needed
you were nothing close
to what i deserved

everything was nothing.

i will no longer search

for my everything

in a relationship with someone

who does nothing to keep me

this love of self.

deeply and truly
i love me, so much

April 5th I.

talking shit about others

won't reduce the shit

in your life

April 5th II.

listen and understand

you will need me

before i ever need you

and knowing this is my power

no suffering.

i don't suffer from OCD

i thrive from it

no.

never apologize

for saying no to the things

you didn't truly want

wounds.

one day

every scar on your heart

will make sense

spectrum.

she is color

in a world painted gray

searching the wrong place.

do not search for comfort

in the same heart

that destroyed yours

never, nowhere.

if you missed me

you'd show up

if you missed me

you'd be here

pure strength.

i have seen true power

in the eyes of a woman

who felt broken

but kept fighting

i have witnessed

a warrior's strength

while watching

a woman survive

22 minutes after forever.

the ink in my pen

swells with the urge to write

thoughts coming together

to create words describing you

stories told beneath the moon

under a desk light as you sleep

tonight reminds me of love

and how much you truly

mean to me

2:03:10 a.m.

i forgot about myself

while trying to remember you

the changes, it's over.

we ended

like seasons changing

we disappeared

into a rainy fog

revive.

i breathe life into poetry

with every keystroke

my fingers in motion

i revive what was thought

to be dead

the bookstores.

every bookstore

is a museum

the keeper of words

the holder of my art form

my thoughts on display

a resting place for my books

march, scream, fight.

no more silence

my voice raised with others

who think as openly as me

screaming yes for gender equality

fists up in solitude for equal rights

from that to now.

how do you destroy

the woman

when you were created

in her womb

give, receive.

teach her that love

is not only in giving

remind her that she too

deserves to receive

a love that doesn't force

her soul to weep

kingless.

she's single

which makes her

a kingless queen

and that's okay

live your own life.

life begins again

once you stop living the way

society taught you

unwanted.

unwanted sexual attention

harms the mind

hurts the heart

and bothers the soul

stop

stop

stop

winter within.

we grow colder

the longer we hold on

to anything that isn't

good for our soul

the mourning of.

wearing the color black

mourning the loss of myself

the fracture of my innocence

the cracks in my heart

silent night.

you asked me how i felt

and silence was my response

because nothing was what i felt

the unconditional.

you won't leave right away

your heart will break

your mind will grow weary

and your soul

will long for more

but you'll reach

for the person who pushed you

to the edge

because you're in love

and that love is unconditional

that love is beautiful

that love is pure

that love should be given

to yourself

more than stars.

while the stars

compete for the moon's attention

she is the only light

that i search for in darkness

wearing masks.

i'm fine

i'm okay

i'm just tired

i've been hurting

the happiness

is the mask

that hides

all emotional truth

and i've been hiding

all of me

from all of you

no. 1 in April.

these words pour from me

like rain from foggy skies

i often fear that i'll drown

in my own pool of sadness

submerged, reaching for no one

because only i can save me

i have always saved myself

no. 2 in April.

what are we

where are you

did you get my call

did you get my text

what do you feel

do you miss me

what are we

where do we go from here

am i wasting my heart on you

are you the one

are you seeing other people

are we exclusive

do you love me

why am i asking questions

that i should know the answers to

why do i feel the need

to question you

and yet you never answer

little Raymond.

and to the Raymonds of the world

the underachievers

who mumble underneath their breath

when in the same room

as the overachiever

i hope you find your way

out of the pit of your own failures

i hope you find some peace

among the chaos you've created

i wish you well

as you continuously defame others

to make up for your own shortcomings

how sad, how weak

love, your love.

it's okay to love whatever

or whomever you love

even if what you love

isn't accepted by others

April in New York.

my April is colder

than usual

my April pours rain

like Seattle

my April hides the sun

behind its clouds

my April is gloomy

like a sky painted gray

standing in truth.

there are times

when i don't want

to be strong

there are moments

when i'd rather not smile

there are days

when i feel like screaming

there are nights

when i crumble into the darkness

of the night

for years i've been fighting

and most days i want to quit

so many years of surviving

and tonight i feel like shit

and i'm not afraid or ashamed

to admit that i'm not okay

i'm far from fine

a long way from being happy

this is it, my honesty

i will stand in my truth

i will stand when it hurts

i will stand even when i feel

like falling

the city of sin.

cigar smoke dancing

in my lungs

the city's vices on display

for everyone to see

the music loud

the people in a daze

high off life's drug

some pretending to be happy

most of all everyone

trying to escape their daily woes

i suppose i'm sort of like them

here in this moment

trying to chase away

whatever it is that's been

weighing me down

i needed to get away

and this is it

me among family

me, filled with peace

6:29:10.

my mind

a museum of madness

my heart

a museum of pain

all the lonely people.

the club was often interesting

but rarely fun

weirdly i thought

the remedy for my loneliness

was to go to a place

filled with lonelier people

the next morning.

the club was just a place

where people were celebrating

their struggles

by drinking to get away

from all the fucked-up things

that occur in their lives

a temporary distraction

from all the things

that will still be there

when the music stops playing

a loneliness that will still be there

in the morning after the stranger leaves

the club has been prescribed

to anyone going through

whatever they're going through

but just as i've found out for myself

the club won't save you

observations in sin city.

there's a difference between
being wanted and being loved

and i realized this even more
while in the lobby of the hotel
in Vegas, a place that also entertained
thousands of people with a casino
restaurants and clubs

i watched men and women
stumble in drunken misery
some alone, others together
finding each other but only
for the moment

i held my fiancée a little tighter
that night

the finish.

to the eyes fixated

on this page

to the heart

that feels broken

to the mind

that feels tired

to the voice

that struggles to speak

to the voice

that struggles

to be heard

to the voice

that the world

has attempted to silence

i hope you found

a truth in these words

i hope you found

the inspiration

to keep fighting

to keep living

to keep surviving

to keep speaking

to keep going

i hope you found strength

in these words

i hope you found something

that'll motivate your soul

to keep pursuing

or going after all the things

you deserve

thank you for giving me

your attention

until next time

keep fighting

keep fighting

keep fighting

keep fighting

index.

a.

t.

u.

a beautiful composition of broken

Andrews McMeel Publishing
a division of Andrews McMeel Universal
1130 Walnut Street, Kansas City, Missouri 64106

www.andrewsmcmeel.com

17 18 19 20 21 RR2 10 9 8 7 6 5 4 3 2

ISBN: 978-1-4494-9016-4

Library of Congress Control Number: 2017939988

Editor: Patty Rice

Designer/Art Director: Diane Marsh

Production Editor: Kevin Kotur

Production Manager: Cliff Koehler

attention: schools and businesses

Andrews McMeel books are available at quantity discounts
with bulk purchase for educational, business, or sales
promotional use. For information, please e-mail the Andrews
McMeel Publishing Special Sales Department:
specialsales@amuniversal.com.